RACIAL JUSTICE IN AMERICA
EXCELLENCE AND ACHIEVEMENT

6888th BATTALION and MILITARY ACHIEVEMENT

KELISA WING

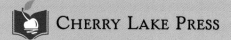
CHERRY LAKE PRESS

Published in the United States of America by Cherry Lake Publishing Group
Ann Arbor, Michigan
www.cherrylakepublishing.com

Reading Adviser: Beth Walker Gambro, MS, Ed., Reading Consultant, Yorkville, IL
Content Adviser: Kelisa Wing
Book Design and Cover Art: Felicia Macheske

Photo Credits: Library of Congress/Engraving by Paul Revere, LOC Control No.2008661777, 5; U.S. National Archives, Recruitment Poster, Identifier: 1497351, 7; U.S. National Archives, David M. Rubenstein Gallery, Department of the Navy, 9; © Military Collection/Alamy Stock Photo, 10; U.S. National Archives, Department of Defense. Department of the Army. Identifier: 175539237, 13; U.S. National Archives, Department of Defense. Department of the Navy, Identifier: 520670, 14; Library of Congress, Photo by Roger Smith, LOC Control No: 2017859749, 17; U.S. National Archives, Department of Defense, Identifier: 531334, 19; U.S. National Archives, War Department. 1789-9/18/1947, Identifier:26431456, 21; © Asar Studios/ Alamy Stock Photo, 23: Library of Congress, Photo by Toni Frissell, LOC Control No: 96507762, 25; U.S. National Archives, Office of Management and Administration. Office of White House Management, Identifier: 5997336, 27; © Visions of America, LLC/Alamy Stock Photo, 29: © Stocktrek Images, Inc./Alamy Stock Photo, 30

Graphics Throughout: © debra hughes/Shutterstock.com; © Galyna_P/Shutterstock.com

Cherry Lake Press is an imprint of Cherry Lake Publishing Group.

Library of Congress Cataloging-in-Publication Data

Names: Wing, Kelisa, author.
Title: 6888th Battalion and military achievement / Kelisa Wing.
Description: Ann Arbor : Cherry Lake Publishing, [2022] | Series: Racial justice in America: excellence and achievement | Audience: Grades 7-9 | Summary: "Black people have fought in every war the United States has been in, even when they weren't able to officially serve. Readers will discover the bravery and achievements of Black soldiers and units—including the storied 6888th battalion of tenacious Black women. The Racial Justice in America: Excellence and Achievement series celebrates Black achievement and culture, while exploring racism in a comprehensive, honest, and age-appropriate way. Developed in conjunction with educator, advocate, and author Kelisa Wing to reach children of all races and encourage them to approach our history with open eyes and minds. Books include 21st Century Skills and content, activities created by Wing, table of contents, glossary, index, author biography, sidebars, and educational matter"—Provided by publisher.
Identifiers: LCCN 2021047048 | ISBN 9781534199316 (hardcover) | ISBN 9781668900451 (paperback) | ISBN 9781668901892 (pdf) | ISBN 9781668906217 (ebook)
Subjects: LCSH: United States—Armed Forces—African Americans—History—Juvenile literature. | African American soldiers—Biography—Juvenile literature. | United States. Army. Women's Army Corps. Central Postal Battalion, 6888th—Juvenile literature. | World War, 1939-1945—Participation, African American—Juvenile literature. | United States—History, Military—Juvenile literature.
Classification: LCC E185.63 .W825 2022 | DDC 940.54/03—dc23
LC record available at https://lccn.loc.gov/2021047048

Cherry Lake Publishing Group would like to acknowledge the work of the Partnership for 21st Century Learning, a Network of Battelle for Kids. Please visit *http://www.battelleforkids.org/networks/p21* for more information.

Printed in the United States of America
Corporate Graphics

All glory to God. For Donald and the ancestors who have served and paid the ultimate sacrifice in the service of this country. For Jadon and Naima. Remember true liberation comes from within. I do all I do to be a living legacy for you. I love you to life.

Kelisa Wing honorably served in the U.S. Army and has been an educator for 14 years. She is the author of *Promises and Possibilities: Dismantling the School to Prison Pipeline*, *If I Could: Lessons for Navigating an Unjust World*, and *Weeds & Seeds: How to Stay Positive in the Midst of Life's Storms*. She speaks both nationally and internationally about discipline reform, equity, and student engagement. Kelisa lives in Northern Virginia with her husband and two children.

CHAPTER 1

What Is the History of Blacks in the Military?

I solemnly swear to support and defend the constitution against all enemies both foreign and domestic; that I will bear true faith and allegiance to the same; and that I will obey the orders of the President of the United States and the orders of the officers appointed over me, according to regulations and the Uniform Code of Military Justice. So help me God.

This is the oath that those who serve our country in the uniformed services take when they join the military. The oath was written in 1789, at a time when there was racial inequality in the military.

Black people have served in every war in American history. More than 5,000 Black soldiers, both enslaved and free, fought in the Revolutionary War (1775–1781). Those who were enslaved were promised their freedom in return for their service.

The Revolutionary War was fought to gain independence from Britain and to establish the American colonies as an independent nation. It is difficult to imagine the colonists fighting for freedom from Britain while at the same time keeping so many people enslaved.

Crispus Attucks was one of the five victims of the Boston Massacre. Attucks was **Indigenous** and Black and served in the Revolutionary War. His death was important in that he died for the United States, even though he had been enslaved previously.

When President Abraham Lincoln signed the Emancipation Proclamation into law in 1863, many Black Americans enlisted in the Union Army. About 180,000 Black soldiers fought in the Civil War. Black soldiers were barely paid enough to live. They were paid only $7 per month, while White soldiers were paid $13 per month!

Even though there was inequality in the Civil War for Black soldiers, they still fought with valor. One of the most famous units was the 54th Regiment from Massachusetts. Colonel Robert Shaw led this unit. Its soldiers made history by being one of the first all-Black units to engage in combat with Confederate soldiers.

Because of the bravery of the 54th Regiment, other Black soldiers were better respected and given better pay. The story of the 54th Regiment was made into the movie *Glory* in 1989.

TO COLORED MEN!

FREEDOM,

Protection, Pay, and a Call to Military Duty!

On the 1st day of January, 1863, the President of the United States proclaimed FREE-DOM to over THREE MILLIONS OF SLAVES. This decree is to be enforced by all the power of the Nation. On the 21st of July last he issued the following order:

PROTECTION OF COLORED TROOPS.

"WAR DEPARTMENT, ADJUTANT GENERAL'S OFFICE,
WASHINGTON, July 21.

"*General Order, No. 233.*

"The following order of the President is published for the information and government of all concerned:—

EXECUTIVE MANSION, WASHINGTON, July 30.

"'It is the duty of every Government to give protection to its citizens, of whatever class, color, or condition, and especially to those wh are duly organized as soldiers in the public service. The law of nations, and the usages and customs of war, as carried on by civilized powers, permit no distinction as to color in the treatment of prisoners of war as public enemies. To sell or enslave any captured person on account of his color, is a relapse into barbarism, and a crime against the civilization of the age.

"'The Government of the United States will give the same protection to all its soldiers, and if the enemy shall sell or enslave any one because of his color, the offense shall be punished by retaliation upon the enemy's prisoners in our possession. It is, therefore, ordered, for every soldier of the United States, killed in violation of the laws of war, a rebel soldier shall be executed; and for every one enslaved by the enemy, or sold into slavery, a rebel soldier shall be placed at hard labor on the public works, and continued at such labor until the other shall be released and receive the treatment due to prisoners of war.

'"ABRAHAM LINCOLN."'

'"By order of the Secretary of War.
'"E. D. TOWNSEND, Assistant Adjutant General."'

That the President is in earnest the rebels soon began to find out, as witness the following order from his Secretary of War:

"WAR DEPARTMENT, WASHINGTON CITY, August 8, 1863.

"SIR: Your letter of the 3d inst., calling the attention of this Department to the cases of Orin H. Brown, William H. Johnston, and Wm. Wilson, three colored men captured on the gunboat Isaac Smith, has received consideration. This Department has directed that three rebel prisoners of South Carolina, if there be any such in our possession, and if not, three others, be confined in close custody and held as hostages for Brown, Johnston and Wilson, and that the fact be communicated to the rebel authorities at Richmond.

"Very respectfully your obedient servant,

"EDWIN M. STANTON, Secretary of War.

"The Hon. GIDEON WELLES, Secretary of the Navy."

And retaliation will be our practice now—man for man—to the bitter end.

In World War I (1914–1918), 350,000 Black Americans served in the military. The military was still segregated.

By World War II (1939–1945), 2.5 million Black Americans had registered for the draft. Black men enlisted, and many Black women volunteered to help. At the time, women weren't allowed to serve in most military jobs.

The Tuskegee Airmen, also known as the "Red Tails," were the first Black pilots to serve in a war. The Buffalo Soldiers also made history in World War II as the first Black soldiers sent into combat. Finally, in 1948, President Harry S. Truman integrated the military.

Black soldiers fought in the Korean War (1950–1953) and Vietnam War (1954–1975). It was the first time that they served in an integrated military, but they still faced a lot of discrimination.

An integrated military meant that soldiers of all races ate together, shared barracks, and served in the same units.

By the time America entered the Gulf War in 1991, many Black soldiers were fighting on the front line. Women were playing more of a role in the military, some in combat jobs.

Black soldiers faced discrimination while fighting in Iraq by Iraqis who targeted them more than White soldiers. Fewer Black people enlisted in the military after the Iraq and Afghanistan wars. Latinx and Hispanic soldiers enlisted at a high number, as they could become citizens through their service in war.

After the death of George Floyd in 2020, protests against racial injustice swept across America. In response, the military has been doing a lot of work to treat all soldiers fairly. They have created diversity groups. They have also started having conversations about the military's racial history and how to make the military better for everyone.

CHAPTER 2

Who Was the 6888th Battalion?

Black women have served in every war in American history. They were builders, nurses, cooks, and seamstresses. Some of them even disguised themselves as men and fought in war.

Cathay Williams pretended to be a man during the Civil War. She told the truth about her identity after serving in the military for 2 years. She later joined the Buffalo Soldier regiment and is the only woman to have done so.

During World War II, women finally gained the right to serve. The Women's Army Corps (WAC) was established. The WAC had women working as teachers, translators, lawyers, cooks, clerks, drivers, nurses, and supply workers.

The 6888th Battalion played a vital role during World War II,
even though they weren't allowed in combat jobs.

In 1944, Harriet Ida Pickens and Frances Eliza Wills became the first Black female naval officers.

Imagine a time with no social media. No long-distance calling. No cell phones. Imagine a time when the only way to communicate was by writing a letter and sending it in the mail. In the 1940s, this is the way it was.

When soldiers didn't receive their mail, they didn't know how their families were doing back home. With men fighting in the war, important jobs like working in the mail room or working as medics were not being filled. A backlog of nearly 17 million pieces of mail was undelivered to service members. The WAC was able to step in and serve in these jobs that were important to the success of the war efforts.

Did you know that the mail is a part of the U.S. Constitution? In war, mail is very important to the **morale** of soldiers. At one time, it was the only way to stay in contact with family back home. The mail is still very critical today, as it played an important part in the 2020 political elections.

Besides the U.S. Army, other military jobs opened up to women during World War II. The U.S. Navy had Women Accepted for Volunteer Emergency Service (WAVES). The Coast Guard had the SPARS. Many Black women joined the WAC because that unit was more accepting of them. The WAVES and SPARS only allowed a very small number of Black women in their ranks. The WAC had 855 Black women serving at the height of the war.

Dr. Mary McLeod Bethune was an educator who created a school for Black girls in Florida. Her school eventually combined with an all-Black school for men. It became Bethune-Cookman College, with Bethune serving as its first president.

Bethune was so important in education that President Franklin D. Roosevelt appointed her to serve as his adviser for minority affairs. She advocated for Black women in the WAC to serve in the 6888th Battalion.

In addition to her work in education, Bethune was vice president of the National Association for the Advancement of Colored People (NAACP) and attended the first meeting of the United Nations in 1945; she was the only Black woman there.

855 Black women serving in the WAC deployed to England to help with the backlog of mail. They became known as the 6888th Central Postal Directory Battalion.

Major Charity Adams Earley was the commander of the all-Black women's unit and the highest-ranking Black woman officer during the war. When the unit arrived in England, mail was piled to the roof. Most of the mail was missing important information needed to get it to the right person. The women of the 6888th had to read the letters to learn who the right recipients were.

The women worked in shifts to ensure that the mail room was open 24 hours a day, 7 days a week, until they got all the mail delivered. It took them 3 months to complete this task.

Major Earley estimated that the 6888th Battalion handled 65,000 pieces of mail every shift.

CHAPTER 3

Military Achievements and Firsts

Black people have overcome a lot of adversity and discrimination to serve in the U.S. Armed Forces. They were willing to risk their lives at a time when they did not have rights and weren't even considered citizens. When things seemed difficult, they continued to serve with honor and made history in the process.

Black people accomplished much while serving in the military. During World War I, the 369th Infantry Regiment was known as the Harlem Hellfighters. This all-Black regiment spent more time in combat than any other U.S. unit. They reportedly got their nickname of "hellfighters" from the German soldiers because of their toughness and bravery in battle. When the Hellfighters fought, they never lost any ground.

Members of the 369th Infantry received awards for bravery from WWI allies, but faced discrimination at home.

France awarded 171 Harlem Hellfighters the Croix de Guerre for their bravery, as well as giving the award to the regiment as a whole. The Croix du Guerre means "cross of war" and was created in 1915 to recognize heroism and bravery. Private Henry Johnson, a soldier in the unit who fought off an entire patrol of German fighters with only one other soldier, received the Croix de Guerre. He was also promoted to the rank of sergeant. Johnson was **posthumously** awarded the medal of honor by President Barack Obama in 2015.

The military includes both enlisted members and officers. Enlisted members of the military go through training and take the oath of enlistment. Officers either graduate from college or go through an officer training course. In the segregated military, many Black people served as enlisted members.

Second Lieutenant Henry Flipper made history in 1877 when he graduated from the U.S. Military Academy, also called West Point. He was the first Black officer in any American armed service. He commanded the Buffalo Soldiers after the Civil War.

Flipper was born enslaved in Georgia and attended college in Atlanta. Flipper was bold when he asked Georgia Congress representative James Freeman for a recommendation to be admitted to West Point. His boldness paid off when he got the recommendation. He wrote several books about his time at West Point and later worked for the Justice Department and as an engineer and surveyor for businesses.

Flipper was court-martialed and dismissed from the army in 1881. However, after further research into the conflict and Flipper's treatment as a Black officer, Flipper was pardoned by President Clinton in 1999.

Becoming an officer was an accomplishment for Black military members. The highest rank any service member can achieve is general.

Benjamin O. Davis Sr. was the first Black U.S. military general when he was promoted to the rank in 1940. Even more incredible, Davis also earned the highest rank of an enlisted soldier in 1899 as a sergeant major. He was selected to assist the secretary of the army in efforts to desegregate the military. He was also the commander of the famed Buffalo Soldiers during World War II. When he retired after 50 years of military service, President Truman honored him during the ceremony.

In the military, the position of general includes four ranks. These are brigadier general (one star), major general (two star), lieutenant general (three star), and general (four star).

Benjamin O. Davis Jr., the son of Benjamin Davis Sr., made history in 1954 when he became the first Black person to be promoted to brigadier general in the U.S. Air Force. He was the commander of the famed Buffalo Soldiers during World War II.

Davis Jr. graduated from West Point in 1936 and commanded the Tuskegee Airmen in 1942. President Bill Clinton promoted him to four-star general in 1998 for his distinguished service.

In 1982, General Roscoe Robinson Jr. became the first Black currently serving military member to be promoted to four-star general.

The Tuskegee Airmen were elite fighter pilots in World War II. They were often called "Red Tails."

General Colin Powell made history in 1989 as the first Black chairman of the Joint Chiefs of Staff. The chairman of the Joint Chiefs of Staff is the highest-ranking person in all of the armed services. After his time as the chairman, Powell made history again becoming the first Black secretary of state.

Many Black service members who have made history attended West Point, but they faced discrimination at the prestigious university. Simone Askew made history in 2017 when she became West Point's first Black woman to be the First Captain. The First Captain is the highest-ranking cadet officer at a military school. There have been only nine Black First Captains at West Point.

Lloyd Austin, a retired army four-star general, made history in 2021 when he became the nation's first Black secretary of defense. Since he took over the job, he has worked to make the military and the Department of Defense a more inclusive and welcoming environment.

Colin Powell served as secretary of state under President George W. Bush from 2001 until 2005.

CHAPTER 4

The Military Today

Today people from all walks of life serve in our armed forces. However, the military still has work to do to address racial injustices.

The military still doesn't have many officers of color. There have been efforts to ensure racial and social justice in the military after the protests following the murder of George Floyd. The military has begun more open conversations, surveys, and groups to create change for all soldiers.

As American citizens demand social justice for Black people, the military must also work to let all races serve with fairness and justice.

In spite of the challenges, Black people have served in the armed forces for more than 200 years with honor, valor, and heroism. They will continue this honorable service in the future.

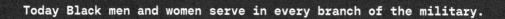

Today Black men and women serve in every branch of the military.

Making a Way Out of NO WAY!!!

Journaling Your Way to Justice!

Have you ever heard of a vision board? People create vision boards to set goals for their future. You can do the same thing by creating a Justice Journal! In your Justice Journal, you can write your way to a better future for everyone.

Start by taking a notebook and adding things to the cover that represent the kind of world you want to see. You can use magazine clippings, crayons, markers, colored pencils, or words. Just be creative in designing your Justice Journal. It's a place where you will write about the world you want to see and then make a plan to create it!

As we have learned, Black people have made significant contributions in the U.S. military in the face of adversity. They still served the country, some even sacrificing their lives, in the name of freedom. Some of their contributions were ignored or taken for granted.

Are there people who do not get recognition or acknowledgment for the work they do? What can you do about it? How can you honor them?

Write or draw in your Justice Journal and create a plan for identifying the problem, coming up with possible solutions, and involving others in the plan to make a change!

EXTEND YOUR LEARNING

Myers, Walter Dean. *The Harlem Hellfighters: When Pride Met Courage*. New York, NY: Harper Collins, 2006.

Weatherford, Carole Boston. *You Can Fly: The Tuskegee Airmen*. New York, NY: Atheneum Books for Young Readers, 2016.

GLOSSARY

allegiance (uh-LEE-juhnss) loyalty or commitment of a subordinate to a superior or of an individual to a group or cause

cadet (kuh-DEHT) a young trainee in the armed services or police force

deployed (dih-PLOYD) moved troops or equipment into position for military action

enlisted (in-LIS-tuhd) joined the military

front line (FRONT LYNE) the military line or part of an army that is closest to the enemy

Indigenous (in-DIH-juh-nuhss) originating or occurring naturally in a particular place; native

integrated (IN-tuh-gray-tuhd) including all races

morale (muh-RAHL) confidence, enthusiasm, and discipline of a person or group at a particular time

officers (AH-fuh-suhrz) people who hold positions of command or authority in the armed services

posthumously (PAHS-chuh-muhs-lee) occurring, awarded, or appearing after a death

prestigious (preh-STIH-juhss) inspiring respect and admiration; having high status

segregated (SEH-grih-GAY-tuhd) legal separation of Black and White citizens in public places such as restaurants, schools, and parks; also known as apartheid

valor (vah-LUHR) great courage in the face of danger, especially in battle

INDEX